EVERYDAY VEGAN PALEO

Tantalize your Taste Buds with Mouth Watering Recipes

Disclaimer

The ideas, concepts and opinions expressed in this book are intended to be used for educational purposes only. This book is provided with the understanding that the authors and publishers are not rendering medical advice of any kind, nor is this book intended to replace medical advice, nor to diagnose, prescribe or treat any disease, condition, illness or injury.

It is imperative that before beginning any diet or exercise program, you receive full medical clearance from a licensed physician. Author and publisher claim no responsibility to any person or entity for any liability, loss, or damage caused or alleged to be caused directly or indirectly as a result of the use, application or interpretation of the material in this book.

Summary

Do you want to live a healthy lifestyle, yet eat all the delicious food that life has to offer? Are you a vegetarian who's looking for healthy recipes that are easy to make at home? Are you searching for quick to make Paleo vegan recipes that will make your day perfect? Well then, you've landed on the right eBook!

Whether you're an amateur, a home based cook, or a person looking for new recipes to try out, you can cook delectable food by following the recipes provided in this book. Cooking has never been this easy. These recipes will enable you to make restaurant quality food that will leave you wanting more. Read on to start on a culinary adventure that's healthy, mouth watering and makes cooking fun.

Contents

Benefits of a Paleo Diet

Paleo diet is said to become the next "Big Thing". What is it? It is the caveman diet or in layman's term; going back to the root of pure and healthy living. Paleolithic diet enables a person to enjoy the delectable foodie delights while providing health benefits at the same time.

Research has proven time and again that Paleo diet improves the living standard of a human being and improves their immune system. Even short consumption of Paleo diet significantly improves your blood pressure, glucose tolerance and lipid profile without resulting in weight loss.

Paleo diet has become a form of dieting that many are not yet aware of. For people who want to reduce weight while living healthy, this diet provides the optimal solution. It is tasty, cuts down on fats and lets the person eat everything they want.

When following a Paleo diet you are eating natural food that is free from any preservatives or hidden sugars. It is rich in nutrients that provides the person following a Paleo diet sustained weight loss and makes them more active and fit to follow a healthy lifestyle. With intake of Paleo diet, there is no need to worry about fats entering your body because they are all healthy for you. You no longer eat anything that will harm you or make you obese.

Quick and Easy Paleo Recipes for Vegans

For vegetable lovers there are wide varieties of Paleo diet options they can choose from. Vegetarians, who want to follow a Paleo diet, can do so with ease. There are thousands of recipes out there that they can follow. However, this eBook provides you the ultimate combination of recipes that are healthy, filled with flavor and all about the vegan lifestyle. Coming up are everyday recipes that are quick and easy to make and heavenly to eat.

Recipes for Breakfast

Tired of following the same old routine? Want to add something new to your breakfast every day? Then peruse on to find out the delightful recipes that are to come in the following pages. Start your day with a healthy breakfast that you just can't wait to whip up every day!

Coconut Pancakes

While thinking of whipping up breakfast, the first thing that pops in your head is Pancakes. Well here is a quick and easy recipe for making gluten free pancakes that are just divine.

Serves: 4

Nutritional Value: Calories: 220, Fat: 16 gm, Carbs: 13 gm, Protein: 8 gm

Ingredients

½ cup organic buckwheat flour

½ cup organic coconut flour

½ cup desiccated coconut

2 tsp gluten free baking powder (heaped)

1 tbsp grounded cinnamon

1 tbsp organic Almond butter

3 ½ cup low fat, coconut milk

½ cup coconut sugar

Coconut oil

Shredded coconut flakes

Berries (of your choice), banana and maple syrup

Directions

1. Preheat a non-stick pan over high heat.
2. Combine the buckwheat flour, coconut flour and baking powder in a large bowl after sifting it thoroughly to get rid of any coarse particles.
3. Add the powdered cinnamon and desiccated coconut, and mix it through.

4. Take another bowl, pour the coconut milk, add almond butter and coconut sugar to it and mix well.
5. Pour the liquid mixture in the dry ingredients little by little. Keep whisking while pouring and making sure to whisk away any lumps that may arise. The consistency of the batter will be thick.
6. Lower the heat of the pan and drizzle coconut oil on it.
7. Take a big serving spoon and ladle one onto the pan.
8. Cook one side for 2-3 minutes till golden brown and then flip and do the same for the other side.
9. Once cooked, take it out and place it on a serving plate. Keep the plate ion a warm place.
10. Follow the same procedure for the rest of the batter.
11. Once all pancakes are cooked, serve them topped with berries, bananas and coconut flakes, drizzled with maple syrup.

Chia, Hemp and Almond Pancakes

Serves: 8

Nutritional Value: Calories: 200, Fat: 12 gm, Carbs: 16 gm, Protein: 12 gm

Ingredients

4 cups chia and hemp cereal, all natural

4 cups almonds flour

2 tsp baking powder

4 bananas, ripe

2 lemon's juice

2 tsp pure vanilla extract

2 packet stevia extract

Directions

1. Add almond flour, chia and hemp cereal and baking powder in a food processor, pulse and set aside. then add in the bananas, a cup of warm water, vanilla extract, and lemon juice.
2. pulse until all the ingredients have combined into a smooth batter. pour the mixture into a mixing bowl, and then ladle a large spoonful of the batter on to a non stick pan on medium high heat. give each side a few minutes until golden brown, and then take it off on to a plate.
3. Follow the same procedure until all the batter has been completely utilized.
4. Let them cool, and serve with sliced bananas.

Coconut Smoothie with Strawberries

Serves: 1

Nutritional Value: Calories: 380, Fat: 3 gm, Carbs: 0 gm, Protein: 1 gm

Ingredients

1 cup fresh or frozen strawberries

¼ cup coconut milk

1 banana

¾ cup water

Directions

Blend all the ingredients together until light and frothy. Pour in a glass and enjoy!

Tofu Scramble with Spinach and Mushrooms

Serves: 8

Nutritional Value: Calories: 270, Fat: 12 gm, Carbs: 18 gm, Protein: 23 gm

Ingredients

2 lb firm tofu, drained

4 cups mushrooms, coarsely chopped

6 roma tomatoes, chopped

4 cups spinach, fresh

2 avocados, coarsely chopped

1 cup sundried tomatoes

2 onions, small in size and finely chopped

6 garlic cloves, finely chopped

4 tsp cumin, grinded

4 tbsp nutritional yeast

2 tsp paprika powder

A pinch of cayenne pepper

2 tbsp of fresh rosemary, finely chopped

½ cup water

2 tbsp coconut oil

2 tbsp each of mustard powder, and soy sauce

Sriracha sauce, to taste

Salt and pepper, to taste

Directions

1. Add cumin, paprika, soy sauce, and yeast, in a small bowl and combine them together until well mixed. break the tofu into bite sized chunks.
2. In a large pan on medium heat, add a tbsp of olive oil or coconut oil, and then add the garlic, sauté it for a minute, then add in the mushrooms and rosemary. Keep sautéing for 5 minutes. use a spatula to prevent the ingredients from breaking further.
3. Add tofu and sauté the mixture for an additional two minutes. then add in the yeast, soy sauce, mustard, and the spice mixture cook for another 5 minutes, lastly add in the roma tomatoes, sauté it for another minute and then transfer it onto a serving platter, and enjoy.

Italian Style Baked Tofu

Serves: 4

Nutritional Value: Calories: 204, Fat: 11 gms , Carbs: 11 gms, Protein: 13 gms

Ingredients

4 cup tomato paste

1 cup puree tofu

¼ cup grated parmesan

Finely chopped Parsley (handful bunch)

1 small loaf of crusty bread

Directions

1. Ladle half of the tomato paste in a baking dish about 6" long, add the tofu on top of it, and pour the remaining sauce on the sides of the tofu.
2. Sprinkle the finely grated parmesan on the top of the tofu.
3. Preheat the oven at 350ºF and place the baking dish in the oven for 4-7 minutes until the tofu just start to set and the cheese completely melts.
4. Take it out and serve it hot, topped with parsley and sliced bread

Banana Nut Porridge

Serves: 4

Nutritional Value: Calories: 140, Fat: 2 gms , Carbs: 27 gms, Protein: 3 gms

Ingredients

½ cup Cashew nuts

½ cup Almonds

½ cup Pecans

1 banana

2 cup coconut milk

2 tsp cinnamon powder

Salt (to taste)

Directions

1. Put the nuts in a large bowl, sprinkle with salt and fill it with water, enough to cover the nuts by 1 inch of water. Let it sit overnight.
2. Drain the nuts, rinse 2-3 times until the water is completely clear.
3. Blend the nuts together with banana, coconut milk and cinnamon until it reaches a smooth consistency.
4. Pour all of this mixture in a pot on medium heat for 5 minutes until warm.
5. Serve in a bowl along with raisins and additional milk if you want.

Blue Berry French toast Casserole

Serves: 6

Nutritional Value: Calories: 240, Fat: 12 gm, Carbs: 20 gm, Protein: 17 gm

Ingredients

1 loaf of Paleo Bread

1 cup blueberries (fresh or frozen)

4 ¼ cup of pureed tofu¼ cup honey

1 cup coconut milk

1 tsp cinnamon powder

1tbsp vanilla extract

Directions

1. Slice the Paleo bread in 1 inch cubes.
2. Line the bread slices in a ramekin or flat baking dish and place the blueberries on top.
3. In a mixing bowl, pour in the coconut milk, add the honey, pureed tofu, cinnamon and vanilla extract and beat gently until all the ingredients are mixed together.
4. Pour this mixture on top of the bread and blueberries.
5. Pre heat the oven at 350°, put the baking dish in the oven and bake at slow heat for 40-45 minutes.
6. Remove from the oven and allow it to rest for 15 minutes. It will set in this amount of time.
7. Cut out and serve.

Breakfast Bars

Serves: 12

Nutritional Value: Calories: 120, Fat: 7 gm, Carbs: 10 gm, Protein: 2 gm

Ingredients

1 cup pumpkin seeds

2 cups almonds

1 cup raisins

1 cup macadamia nuts

1 tbsp vanilla extract

½ tsp sea salt

½ tsp cinnamon powder

Directions

1. Take a large bowl, take out the nuts and seeds in it, cover the contents with water and let them soak overnight.
2. In a separate bowl, place the raisins, cover them with water; around ½ to 1 cup, and let them soak overnight.
3. Pour the raisins with their soaking water in a blender or food processer and make a fine puree.
4. Drain and rinse the nuts and weeds and keep washing them until the water turns clear.
5. Add the nuts and seeds to the raisins puree in the blender/ food processer and blend until the nuts are coarsely chopped and gain the consistency of a granola bar.
6. Add vanilla extract, cinnamon and salt to the mixture and mix well.
7. Pour the mixture onto two large parchment baking sheets
8. Place the sheets in the oven at 250° and bake for 45 minutes.
9. Serve, once cooked.

Cranberry Orange Scones

Serves: 8

Nutritional Value: Calories: 220, Fat: 10 gm, Carbs: 10 gm, Protein: 5 gm

Ingredients

2 cups almond flour (blanched)

¼ tsp sea salt

1tsp baking soda

½ cup dried cranberries

1 tbsp orange zest

¼ cup pureed silken tofu

2 tbsp orange juice

Directions

1. Combine almond flour, salt, baking soda, cranberries, and orange zest together in a mixing bowl.
2. In another mixing bowl, mix the pureed tofu and orange juice.
3. Pour the tofu mixture in the dry ingredients little by little while mixing at the same time.
4. Knead the mixture into a dough and mix well to ensure that the ingredients are mixed well and distributed evenly.
5. Tear the dough into two little circles about ½ inch thick. Cut them like a pizza into 8 slices.
6. Place them on a baking sheet lined with parchment paper and bake at 375° for 10 minutes.
7. Take them out of the oven and serve.

Natural Yogurt with Fresh Fruits and Toasted Cashews

Serves: 1

Nutritional Value: Calories: 125, Fat: 5 gm, Carbs: 3 gm, Protein: 2 gm

Ingredients

Yogurt or coconut milk

4 tbsp of unsweetened low fat yogurt

1 cup cherries (or more if you want)

1 sliced banana

½ tbsp coconut flakes

1 tbsp toasted cashew nuts

Directions

1. Refrigerate the coconut milk overnight so that the cream separates from the milk. If you are taking the yogurt then take low fat yogurt. Deseed the cherries by pressing with a fork or simply making a cut by the side and taking it out.
2. Place a pan on low heat and toast the cashews for 5 minutes or until golden.
3. Put the yogurt or coconut milk in a bowel, put the cherries, banana, coconut flakes and toasted cashews on top and enjoy!

Recipes for Lunch

Now that we are done with some incredibly delicious breakfast recipes, let's move on to the recipes for lunch.

Roasted Eggplant Salad

Serves: 2

Nutritional Value: Calories: 97, Fat: 5 gm, Carbs: 13 gm, Protein: 3 gm

Ingredients

2 cups pumpkin (cut in cubes)

2 eggplants (cut length wise)

2 zucchinis

1 onion, finely sliced

1 cup cherry tomatoes (sliced in half)

2 cups baby spinach leaves

For Dressing

Juice of 1 lemon

3 tbsp extra virgin olive oil

1 clove of garlic (crushed then finely chopped)

Salt and pepper (to taste)

Directions

1. Bake the sliced pumpkin, zucchini, and eggplant for 40-45 minutes in a pre heated oven at 200°, until tender.
2. Take out and set aside to cool. Once they are cool, roughly chop the zucchini and eggplant.
3. Mix the sliced onions, cherry tomatoes and spinach leaves together. Add pumpkin, zucchini, and egg plant and toss to get the flavor together.
4. Whisk together the ingredients for dressing and drizzle over the salad before serving.

Grilled Pineapple Spicy Salsa

Serves: 2

Nutritional Value: Calories: 97, Fat: 5 gm, Carbs: 13 gm, Protein: 3 gm

Ingredients

Olive oil

1 jalapeno

1 pineapple, chopped in big chunks

1 large onion, chopped crosswise to form rings

Baby bell peppers (handful)

½ cup cilantro, chopped

Juice of 1 lime

Salt to taste

Directions

1. Preheat the grill at medium heat. Drizzle few drops of olive oil and grill the pineapples, onions and peppers on each side until a little charred.
2. Take the off from the grill and chop in bite size pieces.
3. Peel the outer skin of the peppers once they are cool.
4. Combine the grilled ingredients in a bowl, add cilantro, lime and salt to taste and enjoy a tasty serving of pineapple salsa.

Pea and Cauliflower Sabji

Serves: 4

Nutritional Value: Calories: 161, Fat: 9 gm, Carbs: 15 gm, Protein: 5 gm

Ingredients

1 large onion, diced

½ cup peas

3 cups cauliflower florets

½ green capsicum, diced

½ red capsicum, diced

1 tsp mustard and cumin seeds

4 garlic cloves, minced

1 tsp chili flakes

2 tsp 5 spice

1 tsp each turmeric and ginger powder

2 cups water

2 tsp coconut oil

Salt to taste

Directions

1. Add the mustard and cumin seeds in a preheated pot, cook till the seeds pop.
2. In another pan, heat the coconut oil and sauté the onions and garlic, until soft. Add the chili seeds, 5 spice, turmeric and ginger powder.
3. Put the cauliflower in the pan and stir gently till all the ingredients are mixed together.
4. Add 1 ½ cups of water, cover with a lid and let it simmer gently for about 20 minutes. Add peas in the last 5 minutes.

5. Add salt to taste and garnish with fresh coriander.
6. Serve with Paleo bread.

Roasted sweet Potato Mash with Baked Vegetables

Serves: 2

Nutritional Value: Calories: 105, Fat: 0 gm, Carbs: 18 gm, Protein: 3 gm

Ingredients

2 tbsp coconut flour

1 large tomato, sliced in circles

2 cups baby spinach leaves

½ eggplant, sliced in circles

2 yellow squash, thinly sliced

1 large sweet potato, finely mashed/ blended

2 tsp coconut oil

Salt to taste

A pinch of cumin

Directions

1. Squeeze the grated sweet potato to remove excess moisture.
2. Grill the eggplant, squash and tomato over medium heat.
3. Mix the sweet potato, cumin, salt, coconut flour, and coconut oil in a large bowl. Take handfuls of this mixture, roll into balls, flatten it, place in a pan on medium heat and cook each side for 8-12 minutes.
4. Warm the spinach over medium heat, add the lemon juice and freshly grinded pepper.
5. Stack all the vegetables together on a platter and serve.

Carrot Scallion Fritters

Serves: 2

Nutritional Value: Calories: 176, Fat: 16 gm, Carbs: 6 gm, Protein: 4 gm

Ingredients

½ tsp coconut flour

¾ cup pureed tofu½ tsp sea salt

3 cups shredded or Julian carrots

3 scallions, finely chopped

Olive oil

Directions

1. Combine carrots, scallion, and tofu and mix together. Then add salt and coconut flour in the mixture and mix until a thick batter is formed.
2. Pour a little olive oil (enough for shallow fry) in a pan and pour spoonfuls of the batter forming small patties in it.
3. Fry each side until golden brown. Transfer the patties on a towel lined plate and repeat the process until the batter is used up.
4. Serve and enjoy!

Zucchini and Hazelnut Salad

Serves: 2

Nutritional Value: Calories: 167, Fat: 14 gm, Carbs: 3 gm, Protein: 3 gm

Ingredients

4tbsp olive oil

1/3 cup hazelnuts

1 ¼ ups basil leaves

1 ¾ lbs zucchini

Salt and black pepper

1tsp balsamic vinegar

2 tsp hazelnut oil

3 ounce parmesan

Directions

1. Roast the hazelnuts in a preheated oven (300°) for 12-15 minutes. Take out and set aside to cool.
2. Preheat a grill pan on high heat. Cut zucchini in long thin slices and dress with olive oil, salt and pepper. Place them on the grill pan and grill each side until charred.
3. Transfer zucchini into a mixing bowl, pour balsamic vinegar, mix well and set aside to cool.
4. Add olive oil, basil and hazelnuts, season well and enjoy.

Kale and Avocado Salad with Almonds, Apples and Nori

Serves: 2

Nutritional Value: Calories: 234, Fat: 17 gm, Carbs: 22 gm, Protein: 7 gm

Ingredients

¼ cups toasted almonds

½ bunch kale

½ avocado

1 apple, diced

1 garlic clove, finely chopped

½ tsp salt

1 sheet of nori

2 tbsp olive oil

Directions

1. Wash the kale leaves, dry then, and then tear them into bite size pieces.
2. In a large bowl, mix the kale, avocado, garlic and olive oil and mix till kale shrinks and tenderizes.
3. Place the kale mixture on a serving plate, top with diced apples and almonds.
4. Soften nori on an open flame, making sure to not let it catch fire. Slice finely and sprinkle on top of the salad.

African Kale and Yam Soup

Serves: 3

Nutritional Value: Calories: 151, Fat: 2 gm, Carbs: 30 gm, Protein: 6 gm

Ingredients

1 yam, peeled and diced

1 small red onion, finely sliced

1 tbsp yellow miso paste

1 cup water

2 cups vegetable stalk/ broth

2 tsp chili powder

1 tsp each cumin and garlic powder

¼ tsp cinnamon

¼ tsp red chili flakes

1 tsp mild curry powder

Directions

1. In a medium sized pot, add onions, ¼ cup water and cook over high heat for 3 minutes or until translucent.
2. Add vegetable stalk/ broth, yam and the remaining water, bring it to boil and reduce the heat to medium. Cook until the yam is tender (3 minutes).
3. Add kale and rest of the ingredients, stirring frequently for 3 minutes.
4. Remove from heat; let it rest for 3 minutes, then serve.

Butternut Squash with Cilantro Vinaigrette

Serves: 4

Nutritional Value: Calories: 121, Fat: 3 gm, Carbs: 15 gm, Protein: 6 gm

Ingredients

1 cup wheat berries, soaked overnight and boiled till tender (1 hour)

1 lb butternut squash, diced

2 cups jicama, diced

½ avocado, diced

3 tbsp lime juice

2 tbsp ground cumin

3 tbsp pepitas

1 tbsp olive oil

¾ tbsp ground coriander

A pinch of cayenne pepper

Directions

1. Roast butternut squash in a preheated oven for 25 minutes until tender.
2. Take out; mix the squash with jicama and avocado in a large bowl.
3. Whisk the lime juice, cumin, olive oil, coriander, and cayenne pepper to make a dressing.
4. Mix wheat berries in the squash mix, pour the dressing on top, mix well and serve.

Pasta with Figs

Serves: 2

Nutritional Value: Calories: 190, Fat: 1 gm, Carbs: 22 gm, Protein: 8 gm

Ingredients

½ lb pasta (boiled till cooked)

1 ½ cup small figs, sliced in half

2 cups yellow beans, chopped

1 can of chick peas

1 onion, chopped

1 tbsp rosemary

1 cup basil, fresh or packed, finely chopped

3 cloves of garlic, finely chopped

¼ cup lemon juice and olive oil

Balsamic vinegar

Directions

1. In a pan heat olive oil at medium heat and sauté onions and green beans for two minutes, then add garlic and almonds; cook till all ingredients are tender.
2. Sprinkle balsamic vinegar to glaze the pan and cook till syrup is formed. Add chick peas and figs.
3. Remove from heat; add basil, rosemary, salt and pepper. Whisk olive oil and lemon juice separately. Add the boiled pasta. Toss it together, drizzle the olive oil and lemon mixture, mix well and serve.

Recipes for Snacks

Can't stop once you start having snacks? Here are some healthy snack recipes for you so you can chow down all you want.

Chilled Vanilla Bean Latte

Serves: 1

Nutritional Value: Calories: 110, Fat: 9 gm, Carbs: 0.4 gm, Protein: 6 gm

Ingredients

Ice cubes

1 ½ tsp honey/ maple syrup

1 cup warm coffee

¼ cup coconut milk

¼ tsp fresh vanilla beans or 1 tsp vanilla extract

1/8 tsp ground cinnamon

Directions

Blend/ mix all the ingredients together. Fill a glass with ice cubes, pour the blended latte in it and enjoy.

Dried 5 Spice Asian Pears

Serves: 10

Nutritional Value: Calories: 210, Fat: 1 gm, Carbs: 16 gm, Protein: 2 gm

Ingredients

½ tsp Chinese 5-Spice Powder

6 Pears
4 cups cold water
2 tsp lemon juice

Directions

1. Fill a bowl with water and lemon juice.
2. Peel the pears and take out the core. Finely slice the pears into ringlets, and put them in the water and lemon mixture as you peel.
3. Drain the pears and dry them on paper. Sprinkle 5-spice on the pears and lay them out in single layers on a dehydrating tray.
4. Dehydrate at 135° for 5-7 hours until pliable and not crisp. Take out, ans set aside to cool.

Creamy Chocolate Avocado Smoothie

Serves: 1

Nutritional Value: Calories: 218, Fat: 13 gm, Carbs: 15 gm, Protein: 5 gm

Ingredients

1 avocado, peeled and diced

1tbsp dark cocoa powder

1 tbsp maca powder (optional)

1 cup Chi coconut water

½ cup almond milk

½ tsp vanilla extract

½ tsp cinnamon

Directions

1. Blend all the ingredients together, until rich, creamy consistency is reached.
2. Pour in a glass and enjoy. Garnish with desiccated coconut.

Almond Butter Apricot Bites

Serves: 1

Nutritional Value: Calories: 59, Fat: 3 gm, Carbs: 7 gm, Protein: 2 gm

Ingredients

10 dried apricots, chopped in small pieces

1 cup almonds

1 cup raisins

½ cup shredded coconut (unsweetened)

1/s tsp cinnamon

Directions

1. Place almonds, raisins and cinnamon together, churn until it forms a thick almond butter paste.
2. Add the chopped apricots, pulse for 30 seconds then add coconut and pulse for 10 seconds.
3. Remove the dough, place on a cutting board topped with plastic to prevent sticking. Wrap the plastic around the top of the dough and knead into a square, 1 inch thick layer.
4. Refrigerate the square mixture for 20-30 minutes. Take out, cut into smaller squares.
5. Store in an airtight container.

Baked Kale Chips

Serves: 8 (15 chips per serving)

Nutritional Value (per serving) : Calories: 117, Fat: 8 gm, Carbs: 11 gm, Protein: 4 gm

Ingredients

1 tbsp olive oil
1 large bunch of kale
Salt and pepper, to taste

Directions

1. Preheat the oven at 275°. Remove the stalks and ribs from kale; rinse it and let it dry.
2. Toss leaves in a bowl, sprinkle with olive oil, salt and pepper, and mix well.
3. Line in a baking tray and bake for 30 minutes or until crispy.
4. Take out, put on a wire rack and set aside to cool.
5. Store in an airtight container.

Walnut Crackers

Serves: 8 (12 crackers per serving)

Nutritional Value (per serving): Calories: 225, Fat: 18 gm, Carbs: 25 gm, Protein: 4 gm

Ingredients

1 cup walnuts, finely chopped

3 cups almond flour, blanched

2 mashed bananas2 tbsp olive oil

1 ½ tsp salt

Directions

1. Mix the almond flour, salt, bananas, walnuts, and oil until it reaches the consistency of dough.
2. Separate dough into two halves. Line two large baking sheets with butter paper and place the dough halves on each sheet.
3. Place butter paper on top of the dough halves and roll them out evenly until it covers the entire baking sheet.
4. Cut the dough in small squares and bake at 350° until golden brown.
5. Take out, side aside to cool and serve.

Fig Tapenade with Crackers

Serves: 16

Nutritional Value: Calories: 225, Fat: 18 gm, Carbs: 25 gm, Protein: 4 gm

Ingredients

2 cup figs, dried

2 cup olives

1tbsp thyme, finely chopped

1 cup water

2 tbsp olive oil

1tsp balsamic vinegar

Directions

1. Put the figs in a food processer and pulse till well chopped. Add water and pulse till a thick paste is formed.
2. Add olives and pulse until mixed well. Then add olive oil, vinegar and thyme and mix and pulse again for 30 seconds.
3. Take out and serve spoonful over crackers.

Nuts Covered in Dark Chocolate

Serves: 16

Nutritional Value: Calories: 240, Fat: 15 gm, Carbs: 19 gm, Protein: 5 gm

Ingredients

Desiccated coconut

1 ¼ cup dark chocolate, melted

1 ½ cup almonds

Directions

1. Melt chocolate in a stainless steel bowl, by placing it over a pot filled with boiling water. Make sure the water does not touch the bowl.
2. Line a baking sheet with butter paper. Put a dollop of melted chocolate at even distance on the baking sheet.
3. Top the chocolate dollops with 2-3 almonds and drizzle spoonful of chocolate on them.
4. Sprinkle with desiccated coconut and refrigerate until chill and firm.

Dehydrated Apples

Serves: 4 (15 apples per serving)

Nutritional Value: Calories: 208, Fat: 0 gm, Carbs: 56 gm, Protein: 2 gm

Ingredients

Apples, thinly sliced (60 gm)

Directions

1. Peel the apples, cut them in half and slice then after taking out the core.
2. Place a piece of baking paper on a flat baking tray and line the sliced apples on it.
3. Set the oven on very low heat (150°). Bake for 10-15 hours, making sure to flip their sides to bake both sides.
4. Once they reach the consistency of a raisin, they are dehydrated, take out and set aside to cool.

Orange and Ginger Smoothie

Serves: 1

Nutritional Value: Calories: 270, Fat: 12 gm, Carbs: 18 gm, Protein: 23 gm

Ingredients

3 ice cubes

¼ cup cashew nuts, raw

Orange juice of two oranges

¼ cup raspberries, fresh or frozen

1 banana, frozen

2 tsp maca powder

½ inch ginger, freshly grated

Directions

Add all the ingredients in a blender and lend it all together until a smooth mixture is formed. pour in a glass, and enjoy.

Recipes for Dinner

So you've had your fill of snacks. Now, it's dinner time, let's take a look at some delicious dinner recipes.

Thai Style Red Curry

Serves: 4

Nutritional Value: Calories: 110, Fat: 8 gm, Carbs: 18 gm, Protein: 2 gm

Ingredients

For Paste

2 stalks of lemon grass

3 shallots

10 cloves of garlic

1 lime zest

1 lime's juice

1 tsp each, lightly toasted coriander and pepper seeds

1 inch each ginger and galangal, peeled

5-10 red chilies

1 bunch of coriander

For Curry

1 cup each, sliced mushrooms and diced eggplants

4 lime leaves

1 sweet potato

1 tbsp coconut oil

2 cups each, coconut cream and water

½ cup green peas

1 tsp coconut sugar

1 tsp vegetable stock powder

1 tsp ground turmeric

Coriander for garnish

Directions

1. Add all the ingredients for paste in a blender and churn until a smooth paste is formed.
2. Heat olive oil in a pot, then add the paste, and let it simmer.
3. Once the paste gets warm, add coconut cream, water and vegetables. Let it simmer gently for a couple of minutes then add coconut sugar, stock powder, lime leaves and turmeric.
4. Simmer till the vegetables soften, pour in a bowl, garnish with coriander and serve with bread or noodles.

Roasted Harisa Vegetable Salad

Serves: 2

Nutritional Value: Calories: 60, Fat: 3 gm, Carbs: 2 gm, Protein: 2 gm

Ingredients

2 tbsp olive oil

2 beetroots, diced

1 red onion, sliced in quarters

1 cup each, pumpkin and eggplant, diced

1 zucchini, diced

1 red capsicum, sliced

½ tsp each of turmeric, cumin, harissa spice powder/ 5 spice powder

4 cloves of garlic, finely chopped

1 bunch each of fresh coriander and parsley, finely chopped

Directions

1. Whisk olive oil, turmeric, cumin, and harissa spice powder together. Drizzle over the vegetables and mix together.
2. Preheat the oven at 200°. place the vegetables in a baking dish and bake till tender (about 45 minutes)
3. Take out and serve with fresh herbs, drizzled with lemon juice.

Asparagus Frittata

Serves: 4

Nutritional Value: Calories: 198, Fat: 15 gm, Carbs: 4 gm, Protein: 13 gm

Ingredients

Salt, to taste

5 mashed bananas, equal in size or 1 ¼ pureed tofu

2 tbsp parmesan, grated

8 oz asparagus, peeled

3 tbsp milk

2 tbsp unsalted butter

Directions

1. Preheat oven at 300°.
2. Boil the asparagus in salted water for 3 minutes, take out and rinse with cold water. Slice each asparagus through the middle, lengthwise.
3. In a bowl, add the tofu, put milk and cheese in the tofu and whisk till the mixture is smooth.
4. In a large baking dish, melt the butter and pour the tofu mixture in it once the butter has stopped bubbling and add the asparagus.
5. Bake for 10-12 minutes, until golden brown, take out, cut into wedges and serve.

Vegan Terrine

Serves: 2

Nutritional Value: Calories: 160, Fat: 10 gm, Carbs: 7 gm, Protein: 5 gm

Ingredients

1 cup cashew nuts and cheese paste (blend cashews and cheese in a mixer, add salt to taste)

1 cup mashed roasted beetroots

1 zucchini, thinly sliced

1 tsp olive oil

2 cups diced butternut pumpkin

Directions

1. Drizzle olive oil in a frying pan, place the zucchini strips and gently cook till translucent. Take out and place on paper towel until cool.
2. Mash the pumpkin after steaming it and set it aside to cool.
3. Line the terrine dish with cling and lay zucchini strips at the bottom. Then add layers of cashew nuts and cheese paste, mashed pumpkins and beetroots and top with zucchini strips.
4. Cover the top of the dish with cling film and refrigerate.
5. Remove the terrine from the dish, cut in slices and serve (at room temperature).

Beetroot Soup

Serves: 2

Nutritional Value: Calories: 125, Fat: 4 gm, Carbs: 19 gm, Protein: 3 gm

Ingredients

6 beetroots, medium size

2 carrots, medium size

4 cloves of garlic

2 ½ cups water

2 tbsp coconut cream

1 tsp each, cumin seeds, salt, and freshly grinded cumin

Directions

1. Preheat oven at 200°.
2. Pour water in a large pot, add beetroots, carrots, and salt and bring it to boil, then let it simmer for 8-10 minutes.
3. Drain the water, and sprinkle beetroots, and carrots with cumin seeds and mix till well coated.
4. In a baking tray lined with parchment paper, add the beetroots and carrots along with garlic cloves and bake for 45 minutes.
5. Take out, peel the garlic. Once peeled, put all the baked ingredients, coconut cream, water and freshly grinded cumin in a mixer and blend till a puree is formed.
6. Serve warm, (reheat if necessary) and garnish with a sprig of rosemary.

Brussels Sprout Burger

Serves: 14

Nutritional Value: Calories: 182, Fat: 11 gm, Carbs: 7 gm, Protein: 14 gm

Ingredients

1/3 cup almond flour

~~¾ cup pureed tofu~~

4 cups brussel sprouts

¼ cup green onions

~~1 cup parmesan, finely grated~~

~~1-1/3 cup goat cheese~~

Salt and pepper, to taste

3 heaped teaspoons 2 + tbps 30g

2 tbs Almond milk 30ml

1 cup Brussels

½ med onion

pinch pink him + cracked pepper

Directions

¼ cup vegusto

1. Wash and finely chop the brussel sprouts. Mix almond flour, parmesan, salt and pepper in them.
2. Crumble goat cheese and mix with your hand to make sure all the ingredients are finely incorporated together.
3. Add the pureed tofu on the brussel sprout mix and combine.
4. Heat oil in a pan at medium heat, make small round burger patties and fry each side until crisp and golden brown.
5. Take out on a plate lined with paper towel and serve.

Spaghetti Aglio

Serves: 2

Nutritional Value: Calories: 140, Fat: 6 gm, Carbs: 25 gm, Protein: 6 gm

Ingredients

7 oz spaghetti

1 ½ tsp chili flakes

¼ cup extra virgin olive oil

2-3 garlic cloves (as you want), finely chopped

3/4 tsp salt

½ tsp pepper

Directions

1. Boil the spaghetti until it is tender, strain it and place in a serving platter.
2. Add garlic, chili flakes, olive oil, salt and pepper, mix well and serve.

Cauliflower Rice

Serves: 4

Nutritional Value: Calories: 76, Fat: 2 gm, Carbs: 10 gm, Protein: 2 gm

Ingredients

1 cauliflower

1 onion, diced

1 tbsp extra virgin olive oil

Salt and pepper, to taste

Directions

1. Coarsely chop the cauliflower, once it has been washed properly, and set aside to dry further. Once dry, pulse in food processer until it reaches the consistency of a rice.
2. Heat olive oil in a frying pan, over medium heat and sauté the onions in it. (add other diced vegetables if you want)
3. Add the processed cauliflower in the frying pan with the onions, mix well, put the lid on and let it cook for 5 minutes. Stir frequently and add salt and pepper to taste.
4. Dish out in a platter and serve.

Stuffed Mushrooms with Roasted Capsicum Hommus

Serves: 2

Nutritional Value: Calories: 125, Fat: 3 gm, Carbs: 2 gm, Protein: 9 gm

Ingredients

Zucchini, sliced

4 large flat mushrooms

Capsicum, thinly sliced

½ cup capsicum hommus

Dukkah, a pinch

Baby spinach leaves

Roasted capsicum hommus (according to your preference)

Salt and pepper, to taste

Directions

1. Peel and wash the mushrooms carefully, then top them with the rest of the ingredients, placed at equal distances in a baking dish.
2. Bake for 30 minutes, adding salt and pepper to taste. Take out ans set aside to cool for 30 seconds
3. Place them on a platter and serve with salad.

Roasted Pumpkin Soup

Serves: 2

Nutritional Value: Calories: 125, Fat: 3 gm, Carbs: 2 gm, Protein: 9 gm

Ingredients

½ tbsp sea salt

2 tbsp peanut butter

1 leek, thinly sliced

1 butternut pumpkin, diced

2 cups water

Pepper, to taste

Directions

1. In a big pot, pour in the water, add pumpkin and leek, bring it to a boil, and then let it simmer at slow heat for about 20 minutes.
2. Blend (using blender or food processor) the contents in the pot until it takes on a smooth and creamy consistency. Add salt and pepper to taste, then add peanut butter and blend again.
3. Season well by tasting it, pour in a soup bowl and serve garnished with parsley.

Recipes for Desserts

Now that you're done with dinner, it's time for some mouth watering deserts.

Hazelnut Chocolate Tart

Serves: 10

Nutritional Value: Calories: 180, Fat: 10 gm, Carbs: 23 gm, Protein: 2 gm

Ingredients

1 ¾ cup dark chocolate, chopped or broken

1 ¼ cup hazelnuts

¼ cup coconut, shredded

¼ cup cocoa powder

½ cup coconut sugar

2 tbsp coconut oil

1 can of coconut cream (full fat)

Fresh berries for garnish

Salt, a pinch

Directions

1. Preheat the oven to 180°. Lightly grease a tart pan with coconut oil and set aside till you get done with the rest of the steps.
2. Put the hazelnuts and coconut in a food processer and pulse until a fine powder is formed. Add cocoa powder, coconut sugar, salt and coconut oil, blitz till a smooth mixture is formed.
3. Press this mixture in a tart pan and bake for 15 minutes, take out and set aside to cool.
4. Pour the coconut cream in a small pan, heat it till it starts simmering, add the broken pieces of chocolate and let it melt until a velvety smooth texture is obtained. Keep stirring continuously to help the chocolate melt and ensure no lumps are formed
5. Pour into the tart pan, over the baked hazelnut mixture. Refrigerate till the ganache (chocolate mixture) sets.
6. Take out, top with berries and serve.

Lemon and Poppy Seed Cake

Serves: 8

Nutritional Value: Calories: 186, Fat: 10 gm, Carbs: 18 gm, Protein: 2 gm

Ingredients

½ cup coconut flour

6 mashed bananas

½ tsp vanilla essence

Juice of 2 lemons

½ tbsp poppy seeds

Zest of 2 lemons

1/2 tsp baking soda

¼ cup each of coconut oil and honey

Directions

1. Preheat oven to 175°. Line a circular baking dish with parchment paper.
2. Add the mashed bananas in a mixing bowl, add vanilla and lemon juice, whisk the mixture until it gains a frothy consistency.
3. Melt coconut oil and honey, then add them in the banana mixture and whisk until well mixed.
4. Combine the coconut flour, baking soda and lemon zest in another bowl, then add spoonfuls of these dry ingredients in the banana mixture one by one while whisking at the same time.
5. Make sure to get rid of any lumps in the mixture.
6. Add poppy seeds and fold them in using a spatula.
7. Pour the mixture in a baking dish (round cake tin) lined with baking paper and place in the oven to bake for 20-25 minutes.
8. Insert a toothpick in the centre to check if its cook. If it comes out clean, then the cake is perfectly cooked.
9. Take out from the oven, cool on a wire rack and serve.

Sesame Crusted Chocolate Balls

Serves: 10

Nutritional Value: Calories: 116, Fat: 3 gm, Carbs: 23 gm, Protein: 3 gm

Ingredients

5 dates, pitted

½ cup cocoa powder

2 tsp maca powder

½ cup almonds

½ cup walnuts

2 tbsp coconut oil, melted

½ cup amaranth puffs

Sesame seeds to roll

Directions

1. Blitz the almonds and walnuts into a fine powder in a food processer. Add dates, cocoa powder, coconut oil, and maca powder, blitz until it reaches a smooth texture.
2. Add the amaranth puffs and stir them through the mixture.
3. Roll into small balls, coat them with sesame seeds and serve.
4. Store in fridge for later use.

Cherry Strawberry Ice Cream

Serves: 10

Nutritional Value: Calories: 150, Fat: 9 gm, Carbs: 17 gm, Protein: 2 gm

Ingredients

¼ cup honey

1 ½ cup strawberries

1 ½ cup cherries

1 tbsp vanilla essence

¼ tsp almond essence

1 can of coconut milk

Directions

1. Blend all the ingredients in a processor.
2. Pour into an ice cream maker and churn the ice cream according to the instructions given on its box.
3. Chill it and serve.

Mandarin Chocolate Truffles

Serves: 10

Nutritional Value: Calories: 150, Fat: 9 gm, Carbs: 17 gm, Protein: 2 gm

Ingredients

2 tsp each of cocoa powder, maca powder and lucuma powder

¼ cup each of oats and sunflower seeds

1 tbsp cocoa butter

2 tsp coconut butter

1 tbsp goji berries

1 tbsp pepitas

Cocoa powder for coating purposes

Directions

1. Melt the coconut butter and cocoa butter in a double boiler over low heat.
2. Add the rest of the ingredients (except the additional cocoa powder) in a food processor and blitz until they form a fine powder and are mixed well together.
3. Using wet hands roll the mixture into small balls and coat them with cocoa powder, then refrigerate.
4. Take out and serve. (These truffles will last for two weeks)

Raspberry Filled Cookies

Serves: 12

Nutritional Value: Calories: 110, Fat: 5 gm, Carbs: 17 gm, Protein: 1 gm

Ingredients

Fresh raspberries, squashed and pureed coarsely with a little sugar

2 cups almond flour, blanched

½ tsp sea salt

2 tbsp honey

1 tbsp vanilla essence

1 tbsp water

2 tbsp grapeseed oil

Directions

1. Take two mixing bowls. Combine almond flour and salt in one and oil, honey, vanilla essence and water in the other.
2. Pour the wet ingredients into the dry ones, while mixing continuously, until it forms dough.
3. Refrigerate the dough for about an hour.
4. Take out the dough, place between two parchment papers and using a rolling pin, roll in out till it is ½ inch thick. Make sure that the dough is evenly rolled out.
5. Take a round cutter and cut the dough into circles.
6. Using your index finger, make an indentation in the centre of each circle and drop a spoonful of raspberry on it.
7. Fold the dough to create 3 sides. Pinch each side to make a triangle shaped pocket.
8. Bake these cookies at 380° until they are golden brown and cooked through.
9. Take out, set aside to cool and serve.

Pumpkin Custard

Serves: 6

Nutritional Value: Calories: 16, Fat: 0 gm, Carbs: 4 gm, Protein: 3 gm

Ingredients

1 ½ cups roasted pumpkin

½ cup cashew nuts

1 tbsp agar flakes

¼ tsp zest of lemon

Sea salt, a pinch

1 ¼ cups boiling water

1 tbsp vanilla extract

2 tsp cinnamon powder

¼ tsp nutmeg powder

Cloves powder, a pinch

¼ cup honey

Directions

1. In a food processor, put the cashew nuts, agar, and salt and blitz till a fine powder is formed.
2. Pour boiling water into the above mixture and blitz until it forms a thick paste.
3. Add pumpkin, honey, and vanilla extract and blitz again until the texture of the paste is smooth.
4. Add cinnamon, nutmeg, cloves, and lemon zest and mix well.
5. Pour the custard into custard cups or ramekins and refrigerate till they set.
6. Take out and serve.

Ice Cream Sundaes

Serves: 2

Nutritional Value: Calories: 185, Fat: 6 gm, Carbs: 25 gm, Protein:5 gm

Ingredients

Almonds, cashews, dried fruit, or any other topping of your choice

1 strawberry, sliced in half

2 mangoes, diced

2 bananas, diced

1 orange, sliced in half and flesh scooped out

Directions

1. Whiz the bananas and mangoes in a blender until a smooth puree is formed.
2. Pour out into the orange halves and serve with your choice of toppings or with strawberry and the scooped out orange pulp.

Vegan Banana Peanut Butter Ice Cream

Serves: 2

Nutritional Value: Calories: 152, Fat: 4 gm, Carbs: 29 gm, Protein: 3 gm

Ingredients

2 bananas

1 tbsp peanut butter

Directions

1. Peel the bananas, chop them into smaller rounds and freeze them for at least two hours.
2. Put these bananas in a blender with the peanut butter and blend them until smooth.
3. Refrigerate and serve.

Triple Almond Chai Pudding

Serves: 8

Nutritional Value: Calories: 127, Fat: 10 gm, Carbs: 8 gm, Protein: 12 gm

Ingredients

6 tbsp Chia seeds

3 tbsp almonds, toasted

2 cups almond milk

 A pinch of salt

2 tbsp maple syrup, pure and raw

½ tsp almond extract

Directions

1. Mix together the chia seeds, almond extract, almonds and maple syrup. Stir them together until well mixed.
2. Then add in the almond milk, and give it another stir.
3. Pour the mixture out in an airtight container and place it in the refrigerator. Let it chill for at least 6 hours.
4. Once chilled, take it out, pour in a glass and enjoy.

Conclusion

If you thought Vegan Paleo food was hard to make, then think again! It's not just diet, its tasty diet. All you need to do is give it a go and try out the recipes provided in this eBook and you'll end up wanting more.

It's Vegan, its Paleo and its divine delicious food that will set you on a culinary journey the likes of which you've never experienced before. Making food was never this easier or tastier. So grab those aprons, put them on, follow the recipes and just start cooking.

Printed in Great Britain
by Amazon.co.uk, Ltd.,
Marston Gate.